CW00557067

THE LIGHT
AT ST IVES

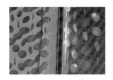

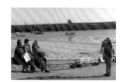

◀ Capis shell curtain 2000
▲ Visitors on the Wharf 1985
▶ Patrick Heron's home,
Eagle's Nest 1987

THE
LIGHT AT
ST IVES

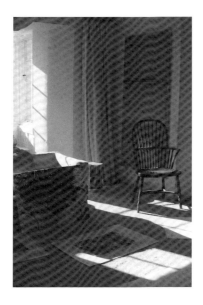

ANN KELLEY

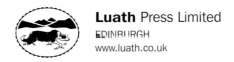

Luath Press Limited
EDINBURGH
www.luath.co.uk

First published 2010

The paper used in this book is recyclable.
It is made from low chlorine pulps produced in a low energy,
low emission manner from renewable forests.

Printed and bound by Scotprint, Haddington

Design by Peter Bennett, St Ives

Typeset in 11 point Perpetua

Text © Luath Press Ltd

Photographs © Ann Kelley

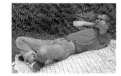

▲Peter Bennett 1984
▶ Sundowner, Porthmeor 1984

To Ron Sutherland, who showed me how to hold a Nikon, load film, and taught me about light. Thanks Ron!
And thanks to you and Carolyn for all the sunsets and sundowners.

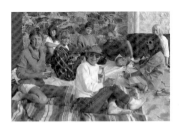

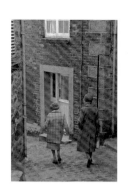

▲ Court Cocking 1984

THE LIGHT AT ST IVES

A myth, he said, set up by the tourist board
to bring in summer visitors, and I admit
I did tend to go on about the light,
but then I think he had a postcard vision of
Hawaiian-yellow sand splodged with red
wind-breakers and bikini blobs, the Island
acid-green against a crude blue sky
and all the colours slipping at the edges.

He probably recalled the jostle and sweat
along the sea-front to the crowded beach,
chips fed to seagulls, St Ives rock,
carved Oriental elephants in Woolworths
and in all the Fore Street tourist shops,
but never walked sheer into the special
clarity of light you find on late September
evenings, approaching from the south.

There is a certain point at which you slip it on
like sea-silk and drift along the Wharf
and up the Digey past the open doors
of houses rooted in deep-sea granite,
between the Bay and the open Atlantic,
washed with cross-currents of marine light
which is mythic and historical and
nothing really to go on about.

Perhaps he never came here in winter
when grey waves beat over Men an Mor
and all the summer restaurants are shut
and the light is the colour of seagulls
flying inland, and the town turns its back.

Sylvia Kantaris

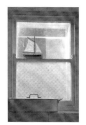

My own introduction to the town was on honeymoon in 1960. We stayed at the Castle Inn in the High Street and spent most of that hot week in early June in the dunes on Porthkidney Sands. A year later, we were living in a rented cottage with no hot water or heating in Street an Pol. My husband, Derek Kelley, was sharing a Porthmeor Studio with Tony O'Malley and a Portuguese painter who was so vain he drew black curls with charcoal on his bald patch. Kelley was painting over Francis Bacon's old canvases. My baby, who had a congenital heart disease, got pneumonia, the cottage was so damp, and we all slept in the sitting room with a portable paraffin heater borrowed from our kind GP (Dr Barwell). It was bitterly cold that first winter, and nappies washed in cold water froze on the line. Not happy days!

I can see those same sand dunes from the house I now share with my second husband. (I spent my second honeymoon in St Ives too. Our wedding party was in our tiny front garden in Bowling Green, but the wind came up so we took champagne and guests down to Porthmeor and watched the sun go down over Clodgy).

Winter light is the best – long shadows march in front or follow you along the white sand beaches; small dogs become great danes; little children stretch into giants. Light constantly changes the colours of the white wooden walls and ceilings.

When clouds are low the light is held in somehow, something to do with mica in the sand, I believe; colours are intensified. And in sunny weather, you could be in Australia or the South of France, Greece, the Bahamas, or East Africa – the water is clear, turquoise, aquamarine, veridian and opal green. At dawn the surf is pink. You could be anywhere but England. But of course the Cornish like to think of themselves as not English but Cornish.

I have been privileged to live in St Ives on and off for over forty years; permanently since 1985. Our wooden house clings to the edge of a cliff surrounded by exotic plants, including bananas and palms, tree ferns and bamboos. Once, an escaped macaw flew across the bay from Paradise Park in Hayle and settled on one of our macrocarpas. It must have thought it had found its tropical home. We have seen porpoises dancing; badgers come to our kitchen door for peanuts; a peregrine falcon has sat in the tree five metres away and torn the fur from a rat he had caught. Oyster catchers, curlews and gulls call in the night.

▲ 5 Bowling Green
1984

In my novel, *The Burying Beetle*, the young protagonist, Gussie, says, 'You can tell where the tide is by the waves on the ceiling.' And 'It's impossible to tell where the sea ends and where the sky begins today. It's the same grey misty haze all over. The crows are grey blurs flying by. A man disappears on the beach, and then only his legs reappear.'

I love the white sea-frets that envelop the cliff some summer mornings. You can see the funnels of mist streaming out of Hayle Estuary, the far end of Porthkidney Sands, and across the bay, blanketing Godrevy Lighthouse and the dunes, and watch as it is gradually burnt off by the sun to leave a brilliant clarity of light.

I am often woken at dawn – 4 am recently – by the extraordinary light, and make the most of it as it strikes our east-facing wooden house horizontally. It was once the cliff-side location in which Havelock Ellis had his studio and wrote about sex. He worked in an upturned boat, and said he had the best view in Cornwall.

Light bounces off walls and ceilings. I wear dark glasses at breakfast and have been known to erect a large black umbrella over my computer screen to block out the light. We have had to paint the inside of the glass roof of the porch, where there is a laundry area, so I can do the ironing in less than tropical temperatures.

Photography is nothing without light, and we have it in quality and quantity in St Ives.

Most of these photographs, some from as far back as 1980, were made using an ancient Nikon FM or an equally decrepit Nikkormat, using only available light. Recently I have been using a digital camera.

In the Foreword to the book of photographs – *Born and Bred*, Portraits of St Ives by Ann Kelley (Cornwall Books 1988) writer DM Thomas says of the town: 'It is a place of many identities… It is the glowing sapphire, catching the breath as its bay slides into sight on a sunny day. Such days are not common enough anywhere in Cornwall; yet in my experience one can often catch at least a haze of sun in St Ives when the skies everywhere else are leaden. 'Let's try St Ives,' we say, when drizzle soaks us; and even if the drizzle doesn't relent, there is usually a lighter, hopeful patch of cloud, which slightly lifts the spirits. So one St Ives is a creature of hope and illusion, poised on the edge of unreality, as it is in Virginia Woolf's *To the Lighthouse*.'

Ann Kelley, St Ives, March 2010

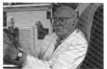 **Some years ago, when I first had the idea for another book of photographs on St Ives, I wrote to several writers and painters asking them to speak of their memories of the town.**

In the early sixties, when I first arrived, the late Sir Terry Frost lived with his wife Kath and six children in a small corner cottage in Downlong, moments from Smeaton's Pier. I vividly remember seeing his energetic and handsome children falling out of the tiny cottage and thinking, how on earth was there room for them all?

SIR TERRY FROST

'We arrived in St Ives in May 1946 to unknown territory, not long married. We had one tin trunk and that had got lost. It contained all our worldly goods including a wonderful cream blanket that had been a wedding present. In its time it had also stored onions for my gran and when it did arrive, having gone astray at Bristol, everything in it reeked of them.

St Ives was quiet, mixed with the instant thrill of the sea, the light, the houses, cottages, narrow alleyways, the sound and rhythm of the Cornish voices, all new to us.

Whilst looking for a B&B we went to the local library to find accommodation and found a caravan in Headland Road, Carbis Bay. Off we went along a wonderful coast path, all space and railway lines with houses tucked in on land sweeping down to the sand and sea at Carbis Bay. The owner of the caravan, Mrs Cave Day, was very nice and agreed to let the caravan to us for thirty shillings a week until it was needed by summer visitors.

We did not know a soul but I found Fuller's Art School. The first artist that I met was Sven Berlin who was sympathetic to my needs and introduced me to John Park and Guido Morris. In Leonard Fuller's life class I also met Peter Lanyon. Everybody was encouraging to me. Life was playing table tennis with Fred Bottomley, working in Keely's as a waiter while Kath worked as a chambermaid, and then painting in the woods and streets of St Ives.

The shock of the light and space, clear air, friendly and helpful people, Porthmeor Beach, The Island, Gurnard's Head, all stirred my emotions; a walk to Zennor along the coast to widen my vision and to feel part of the landscape; the sound of the sea, the visual language of water hitting and wrapping around rocks; the walk along the quay looking down on boats that pushed their mast up your nostrils… St Ives.'

Sir Terry Frost, Newlyn

▲ Sir Terry Frost
2000

BEAUTIFUL TODAY

The banana plants, camellia, echium, wild garlic flower's
rank tang of a more northern spring,
beautiful today the surf on Porthkidney Beach
and the standing out of the lighthouse, sheer
because of the rain past, the rain to come, the rain
that has brought this cliff-side to jungle thickness.

The hammock is green with a winter of rain, beautiful today
the bamboo, wrist-thick. Was it on this
foothold, this shelf, this terrace, it learned
to surf on a hiss of breeze, was it today
that taught this dry handshake of leaves
against the pull of tide on Porthkidney Beach?

A step, a seat, a stare to the east
where light springs from a wasteland
beyond where the wet sun dawns –
beautiful today, sun shakes from its shoulders
the night tides. In a wasteland of easterly light
sun makes play on the waves

but the hollow surf turns over and over
and nobody comes, only a track of footprints
runs to the sea, and the tall pines
make shapes of their limbs – beautiful today
the dazzle they capture as landscape,
the resin they ooze from their wounds.

White planks are full of washed-away footsteps, beautiful
today the graining of sweat and flesh. This shell
wears at its heart a coil
to last when the curves are gone – but today
the flush of light, the flowering of freckles
on tender skin are helplessly present

in the hour between pallor and sunburn,
while the banana plant wears its heart in a fist
of tiny fruit that will never ripen or open.
In the distance, the little town
waits for its saint to sail in on a leaf
for the second time, and bless its legions of roofs.

Helen Dunmore (Glad of These Times, Bloodaxe 2007)
Written after a visit to Hawke's Point

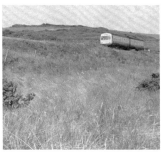

Many people know this part of Cornwall through the books of Rosamunde Pilcher and through the translations and the films that have been made from her novels. Many German visitors come to St Ives specifically because they want to be where she sets her books. When I contacted her about the book of photographs and asked her for a contribution she was generous in her offering.

ROSAMUNDE PILCHER

'I used to go to your house when I was a child. We lived in Lelant. The Shortland Balls lived in Lelant, and I think they built the original shell of the house. They then moved from Lelant to Hawke's Point for the summer, and let their big house to families from London who came down for the summer complete with household staff, chauffeurs, etc! We always loved going there, and going down the cliff to swim and play rounders on the beach.

I was born in Lelant, and lived there for the first twelve years of my life, until the war started and all our lives were torn apart.

But St Ives played a very strong and integral part of our childhood, because it was where we went to school, to Christmas parties, to dancing class, and to shop. My mother had no car, so the journey was made either by bus or by train. The train was our favourite. We lived just above Lelant Railway Station and when my sister was late for school, Charlie, the engine driver, would wait for her, tooting his whistle, while she galloped down the steep path. He was obliging in other ways, too – because we and our friends used the railway line as a shortcut to the estuary beach, and he always sounded a warning as the engine chuntered through the cutting, whereupon we would scatter like pigeons and he would wave a sooty hand in acknowledgement.

St Ives was always an adventure, even if our reason for going was nothing more exciting than visits to the butcher, the fishmonger, or the greengrocer, or perhaps to Martins the drapers in Fore Street, in order to purchase a length of cotton print, which my mother would make up into matching summer frocks for my sister and myself.

Swimming at Lelant was never overly safe, and we didn't bathe there unless there were grown-ups around, or at least a party of older children. But St Ives was different, and at a very early age, my sister and I were allowed, on hot summer mornings, to take the train, by ourselves, to St Ives, and run down the steps to Porthminster Beach. We didn't have a tent, but hired a small wooden changing hut, because modesty was all. There were always people on Porthminster; family parties from Tregenna Castle Hotel, with nannies for their children, and cricket matches and beach balls. There was a diving raft

▲ Branch line to
St Ives 2000

moored a little way offshore, and it was a great day when one could swim far enough to reach the raft, and leap into the water from there. The boys of St Ives didn't swim from the beach, but from rocks below Pednolva Hotel. We used to watch them, hurling themselves from these rocks, and playing other dangerous games, and they probably observed us with contempt, for our lack of the adventurous spirit.

When the summer was over, and the visitors had gone, St Ives, in a strange way, came into its own. Deserted, the cobbled streets revealed themselves, wet after a deluge of rain, and gleaming like fish scales. The wind channelled down narrow lanes; the sky was bleached by the cold. On Porthmeor Beach the breakers thundered in, and the sands stood empty and alien, quite changed from the pleasant place, where in summer, we had ridden our wooden bellyboards on the gentle rollers.

In winter, too, were Christmas parties, and other jollifications, held in the Arts Club, or the Porthminster Hotel. On these occasions, we took a taxi, and travelled in state, bundled into velvet cloaks with fur collars – just about the only time we had the opportunity to wear these impractical and costly garments. I think some Aunt had given them to us, and they ended up, inevitably, in the dressing up box.

Spring was perhaps my favourite time, stealing in early, hard on the heels of winter. Hedges thick with primroses, and the flower farm at Lelant Saltings filling the warm air with the scent of violets. During the Easter holidays, traditionally, we did the cliff walk from Lelant to St Ives. Over the dunes, through the Nut Walk, across Carbis Bay Beach, up Hain Walk below Treloyhan, and so, down into St Ives. A long way for short legs. But the reward was an ice cream, and then the journey home by train.

Many of my mother's friends were artists or potters, as well as older people, retired to the pleasant climate. Mrs Dow, who lived at Talland House, had the same Burma connections as my parents, and Lady White, also retired from Burma, lived in The Cottage, just across the road from Talland Stables. Our favourite adults, however, were George and Kay Bradshaw, both artists. They lived Downalong, in a wonderful house with no windows. I suppose it had once been a net store. Across the street, facing out over Porthmeor, was their studio, and there we used to have picnics with them, and climb out of the window by means of a rope ladder, to run out across the sands, and surf the long, shallow waves.

Seventy years later, with a son farming at Zennor, I still go back. Lelant has changed, but in winter St Ives is yet as I remember it; the streets empty of visitors, glimpses of blue sea at every turn, and all suffused by that brilliant light, absorbed by the sky from the limitless, shifting Atlantic.'

Rosamunde Pilcher, Longforgan, Perthshire

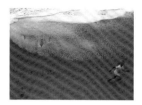

I remember meeting Brian Barron on Porthmeor Beach, in the seventies. I was writing and he was visiting with Tim Llewellyn, another eminent journalist. They were intrigued that I was working on the beach. Porthmeor is the place to gather with friends at the end of a summer's day. You sit against the wall of the Porthmeor Studios, where the warmth is in the granite, and watch as the sea eats the sun.

BRIAN BARRON

'St Ives: the one place on the planet where I always sleep without interruption is here. Usually the window is open and there's the roar and crash of the surf. If there's a westerly storm blowing, the window has to be closed; in winter there might be a ghostly pale dawn then the sky turns slate grey and the gale pounds in, whipping Porthmeor into a frenzy of salty suds that blow crazily over the rooftops. There's a luminous darkness (St Ives is full of contradictions like that) which Patrick Heron and Tony O'Malley, both of whom had Porthmeor studios, caught to individual perfection in their abstract work.

This remains a uniquely beautiful corner of the West Country. Just as I did as a kid with my parents nearly fifty years ago, you can walk out of St Ives towards the Zennor coastal path into unspoilt vistas in less than fifteen minutes. The grandeur of the coast, the fickle nature of the elements, have inspired one of our finest painters, Karl Weschka, who lives here.

On a matchless day in the late summer of 2002 we hiked to Hellesveor and from the clifftop watched porpoises parading past and a lone large seal snuffling around the coves looking for lunch. It was a spring tide and the sea retreated unusually far. We swam off the sandbar then hunted for stones so polished and rounded by thousands of years of Atlantic waves that they resemble cannonballs, small and large.

We succumbed long ago to the siren song of St Ives and regard the community as our home.'

Brian Barron, Rome (was BBC South Europe Correspondent, and reported abroad for BBC TV for 40 years. His widow, Angela, is a painter in St Ives).

▲ Boy on Porthmeor
1988
▶ Harbour beach 2001

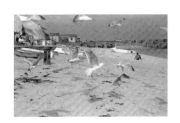

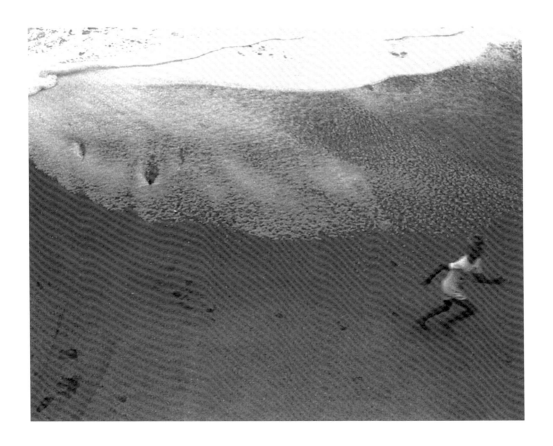

▲ Boy on Porthmeor
1988
▶ Runner, Porthkidney
Sands 2001

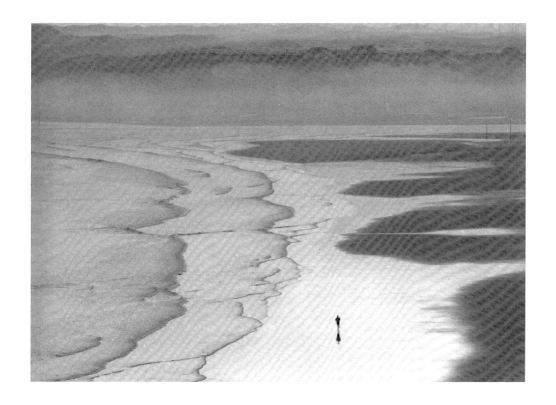

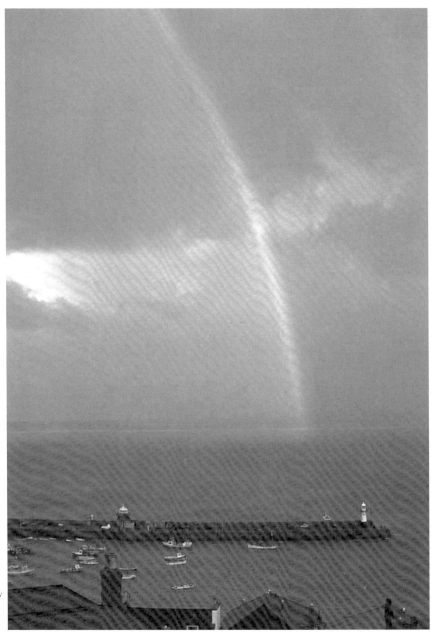

▲ Rainbow, St Ives Bay
2000
▶ Dawn, Porthkidney
2009

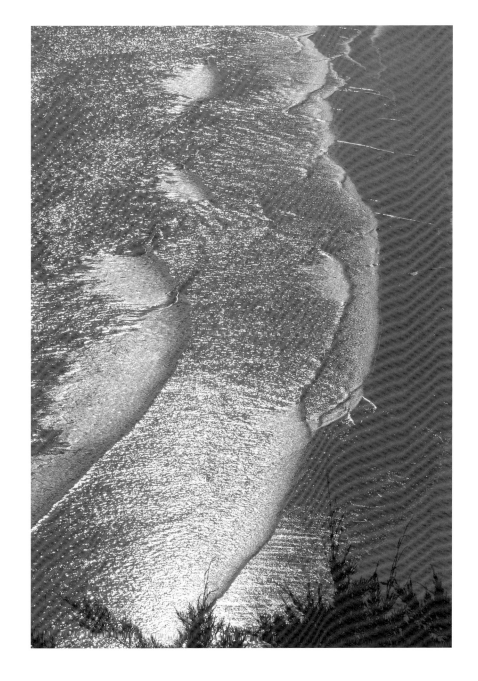

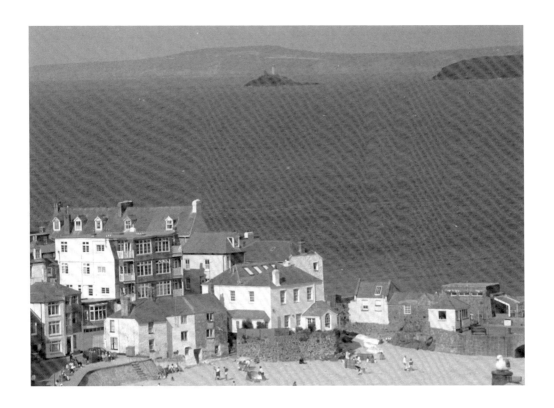

▲ The Harbour Beach
1988
▶ Smeaton's Pier,
Chapel and Harbour
Master's office 1988

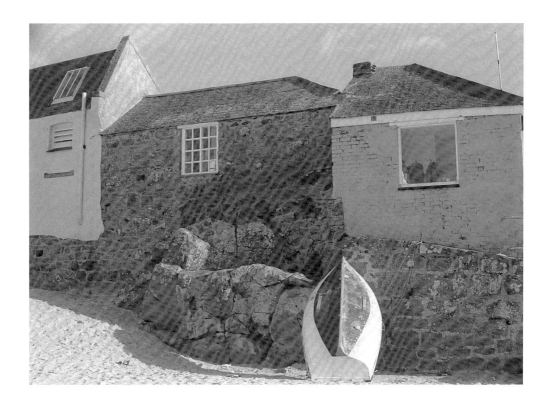

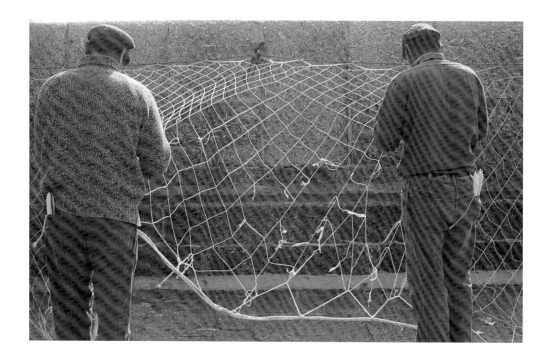

▲ Mending Nets,
Smeaton's pier 1989
▶ Bowling Green,
Porthmeor 1988

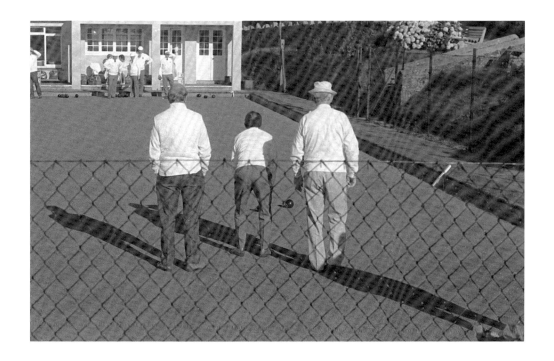

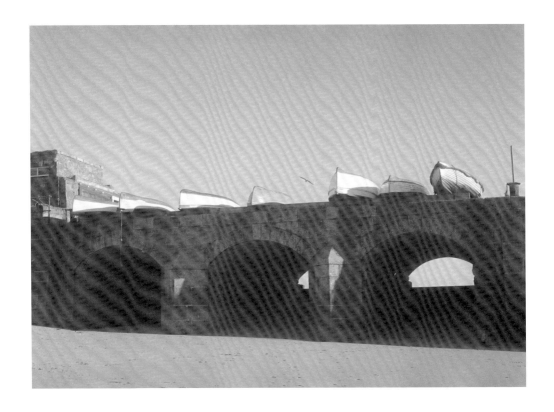

▲ Smeaton's Pier 1980
▶ Sand Horses,
Porthgwidden by
A. Baines 1995

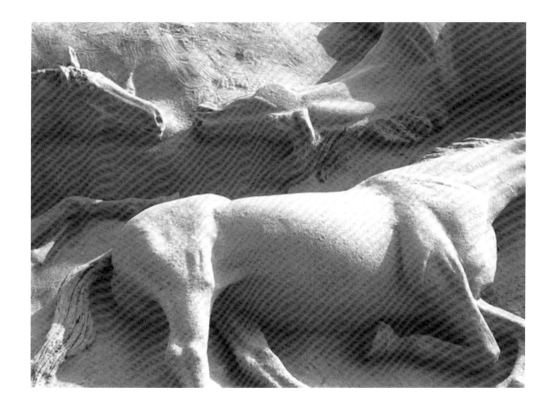

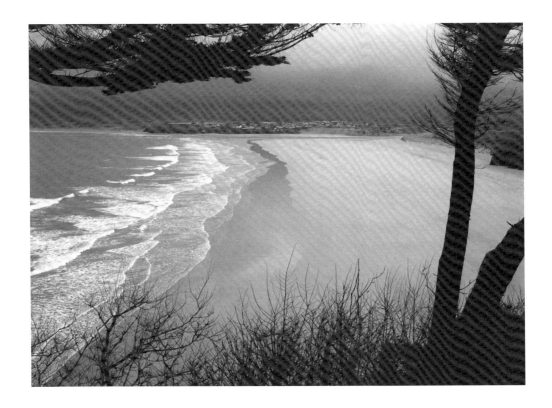

▲ Storm, Porthkidney
1985
▶ Snow, Porthkidney
2009

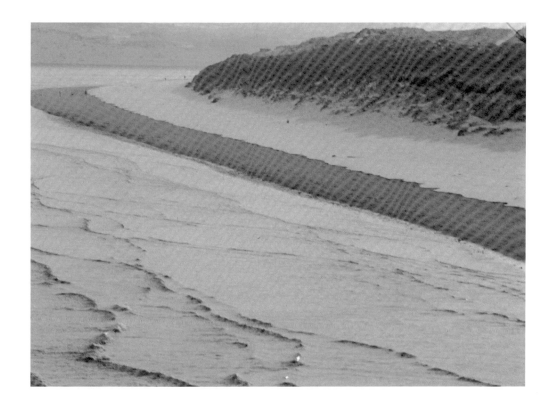

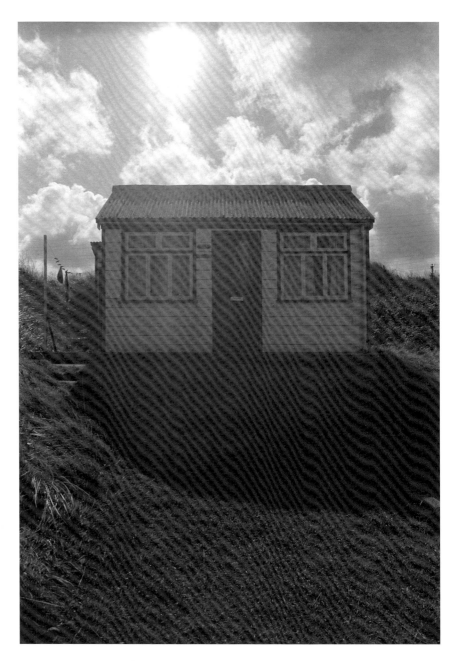

▲ Chalet, Hayle
Towans 1987
▶ The Island from
The Meadow 1985

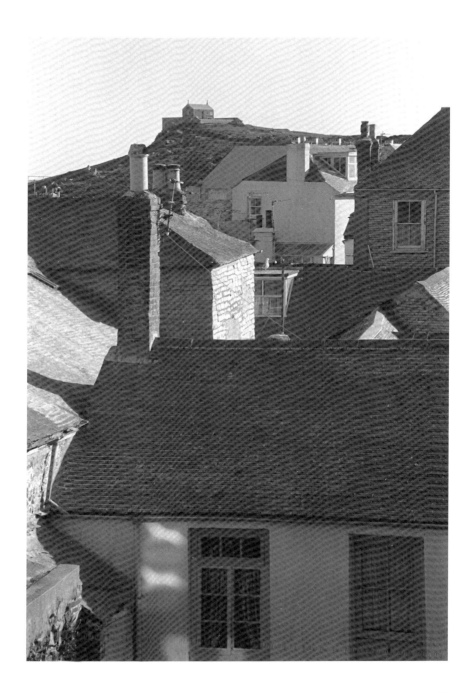

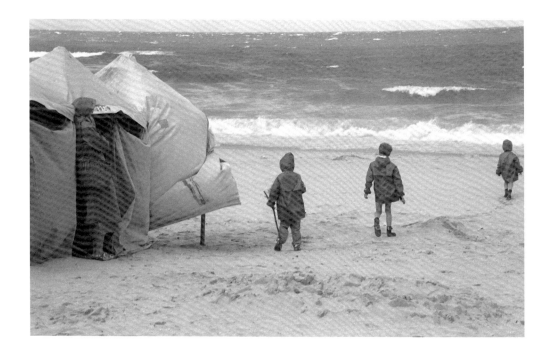

▲ Porthminster, September
1984
▶ Misty Morning on the
Harbour 1984

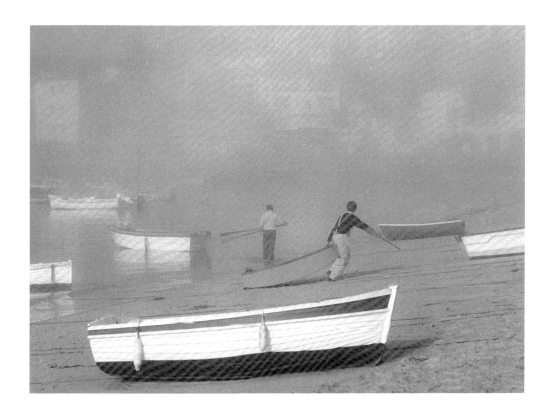

▲ Godrevy Lighthouse 2005
▶ Storm, St Ives Bay 2005

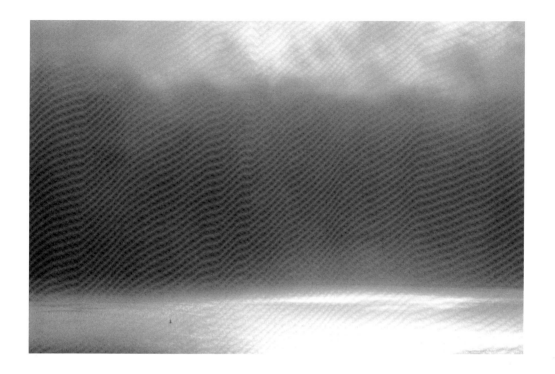

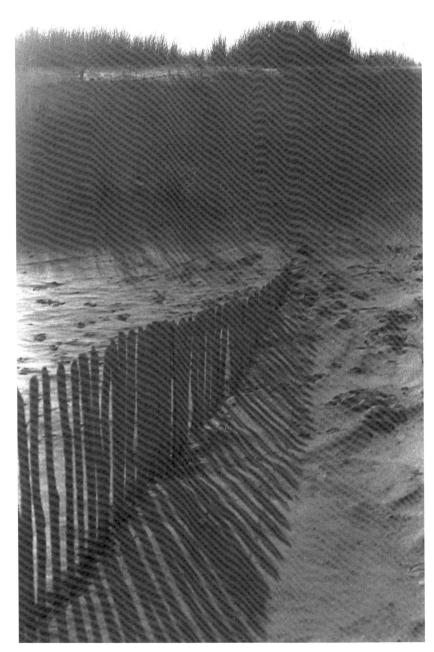

▲ Gwithian Towans
1989
▶ Dune Path 1989

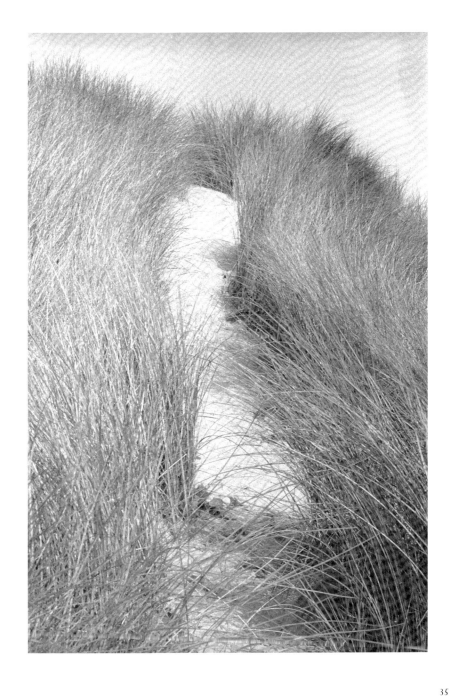

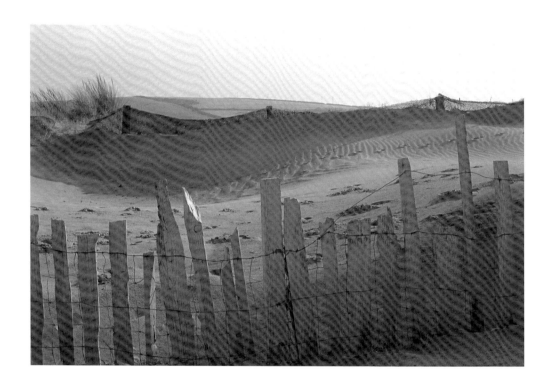

▲ Hayle Towans 1989
▶ St Ives Branch Line 1983

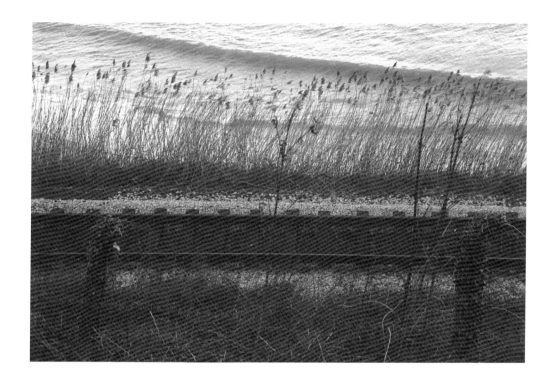

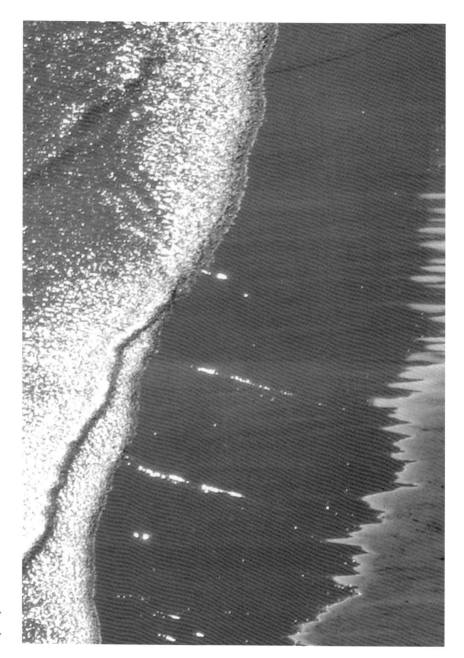

▲ Beach Pattern 1,
2009
▶ Beach Pattern 2,
2003

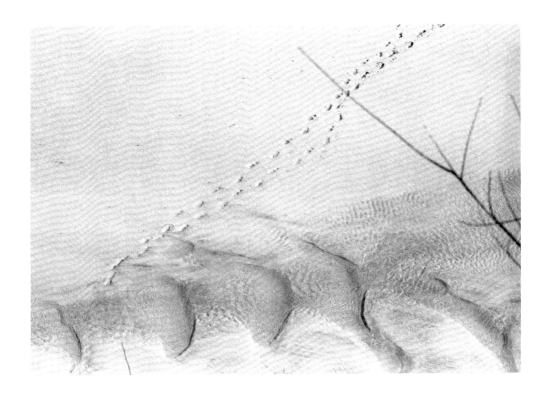

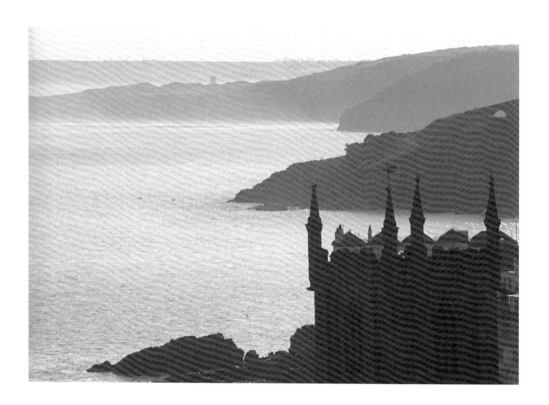

▲ St Eia Church 1989
▶ St Uny Graveyard, 2002

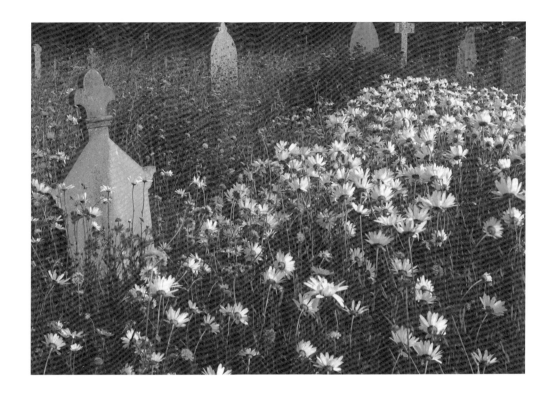

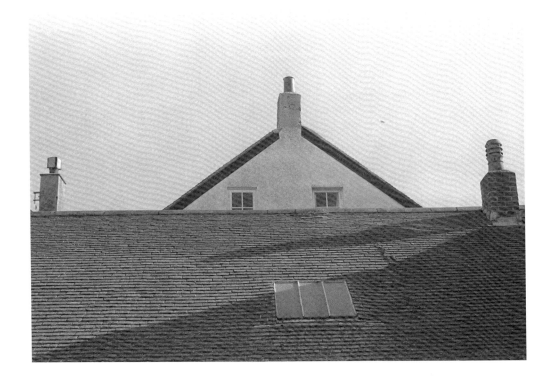

▲ Downlong 1985
▶ Zion Chapel 1987

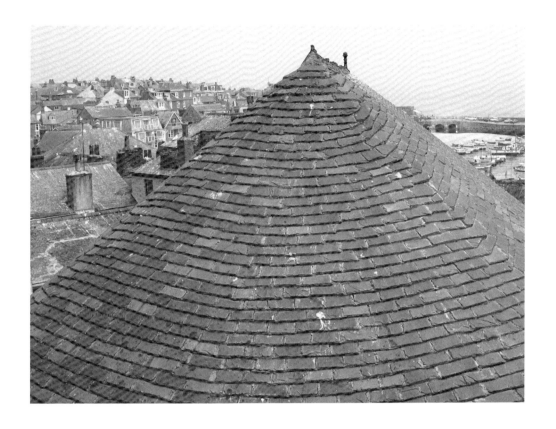

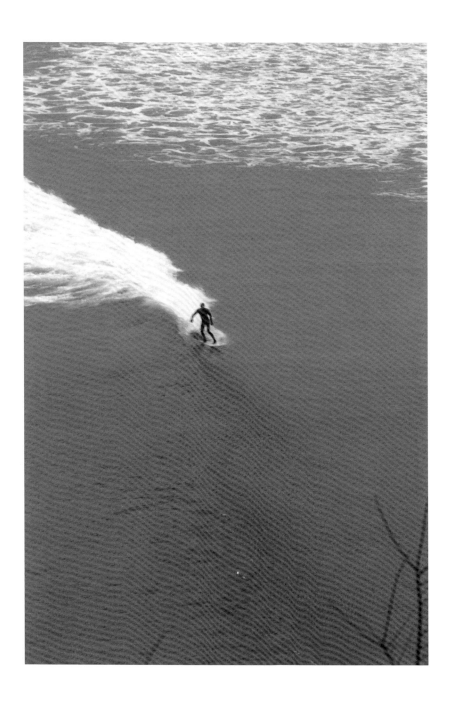

▲ Surfer 2005
▶ Surge 2009

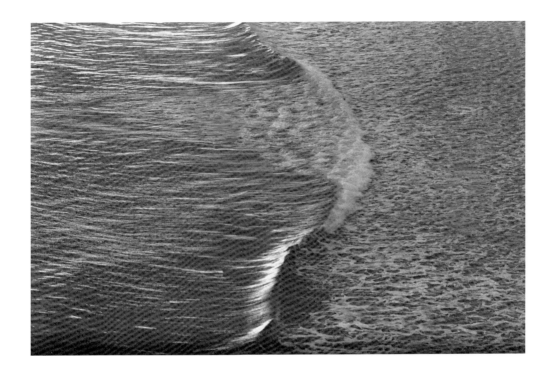

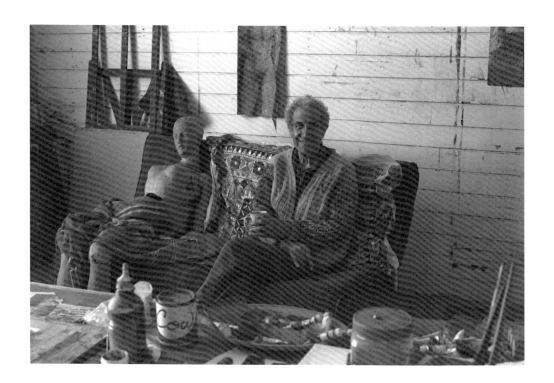

▲ John Emanuel and model
(Gladys) 1992
▶ John Emanuel's
Porthmeor Studio 1992

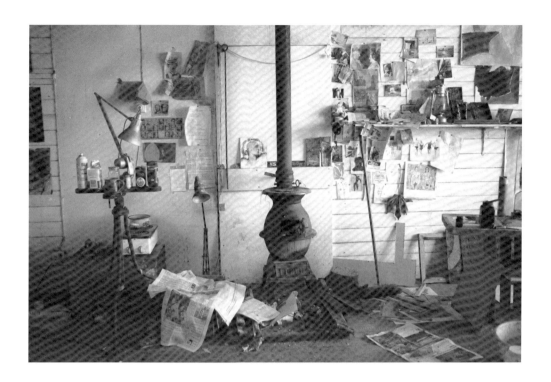

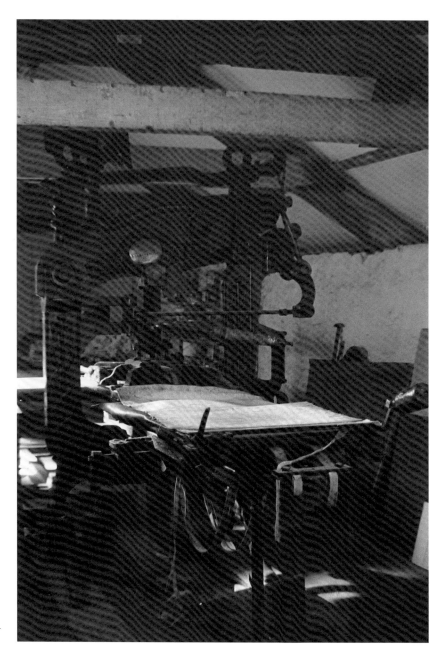

▲ Penwith Gallery
Printing Press 1985
▶ O'Malley's, Seal
Cottage, Porthmeor
1990

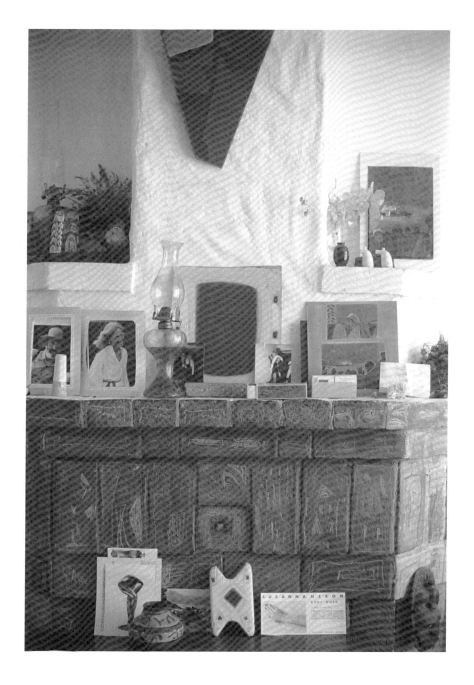

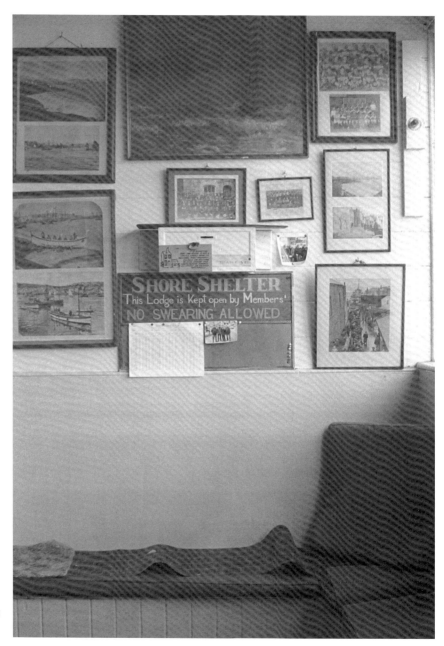

▲ Shore Shelter 1985
▶ 5 Bowling Green
1985

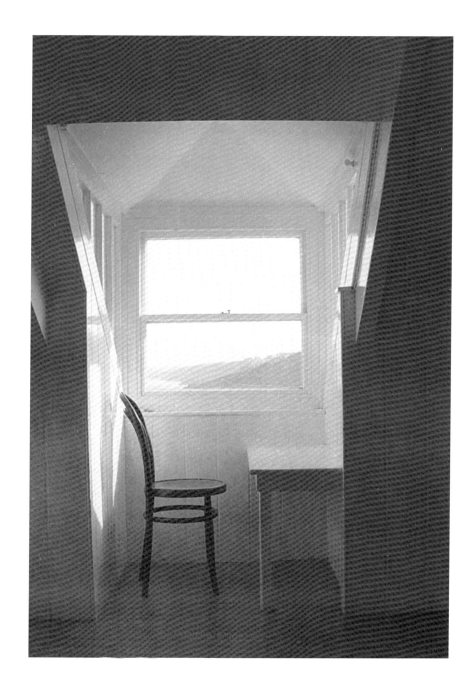

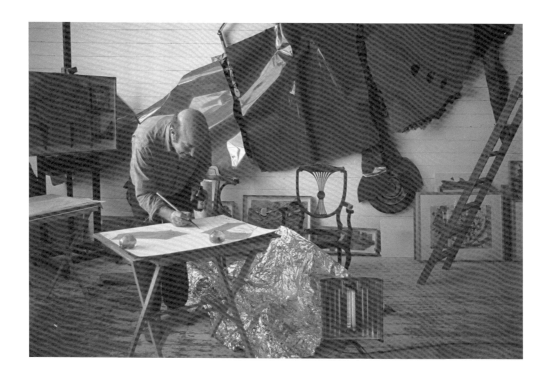

▲ Roy Walker, Porthmeor
Studio 1987
▶ St Ives School of Painting
1994

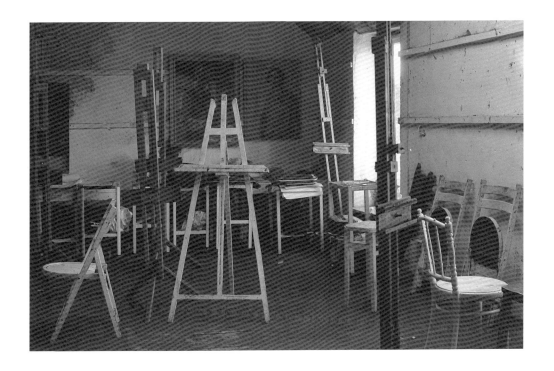

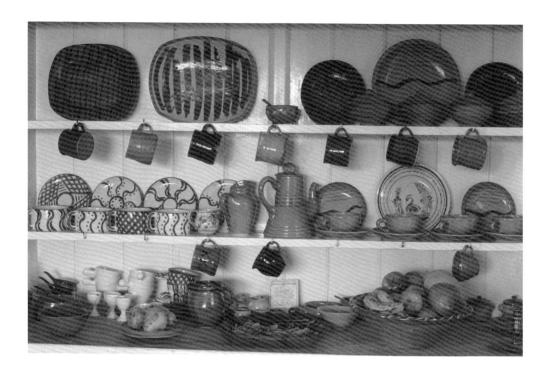

▲ Eagles' Nest – pottery
by Leach and Delia Heron
▶ Patrick Heron, Eagle's
Nest, Zennor

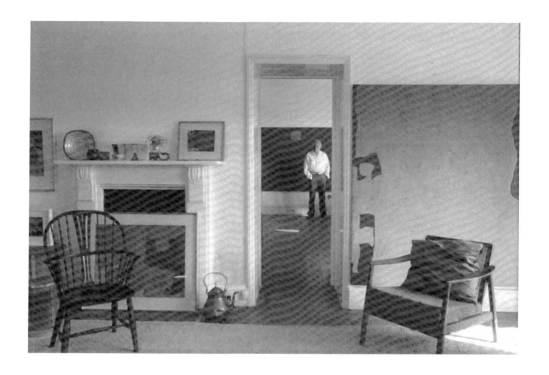

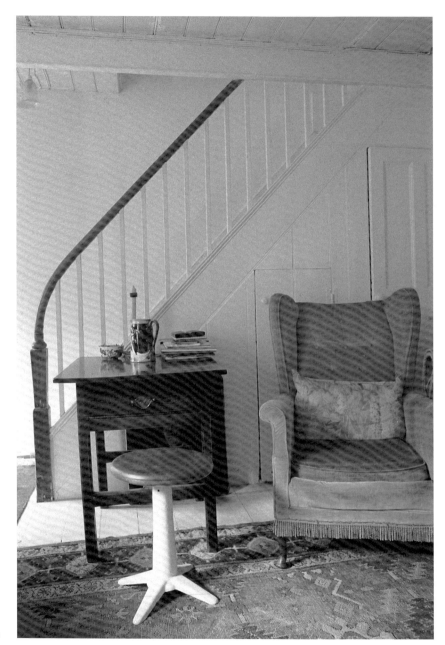

▲ St Peter's Street
1987
▶ Eagle's Nest 1987

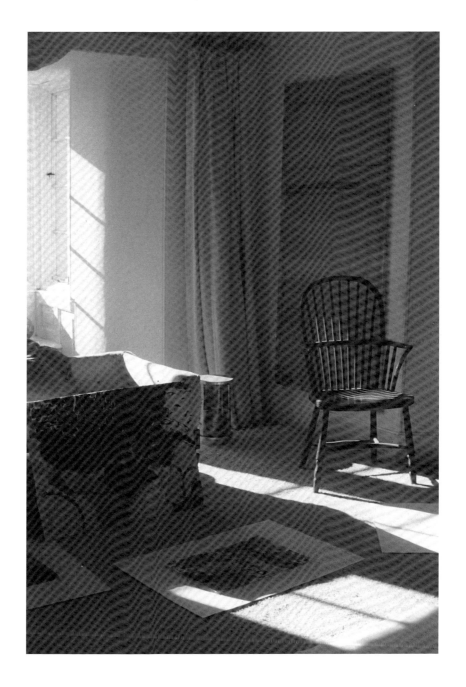

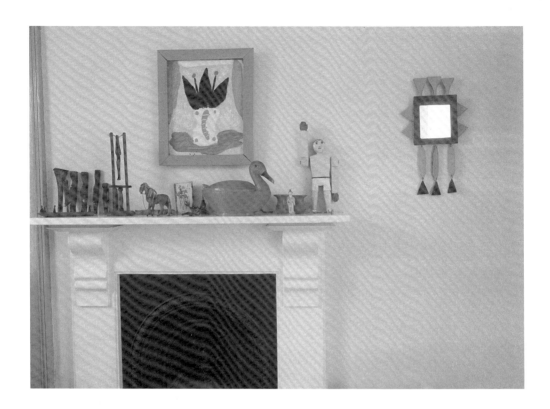

▲ Stella Benjamin's
Mantleshelf, Wooden
Art by Brian Ilsley
▶ Judy Symon's Studio
1994

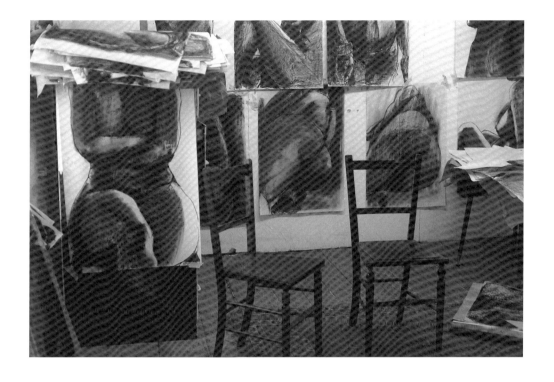

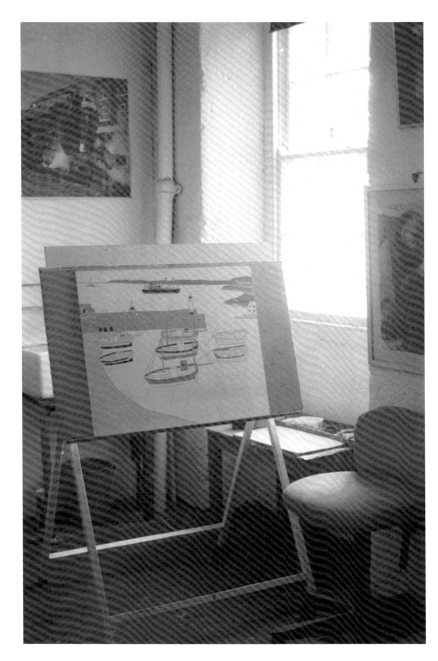

▲ Bryan Pearce's
Studio 1994
▶ Hyman Segal's
studio, Back Road
West 1994

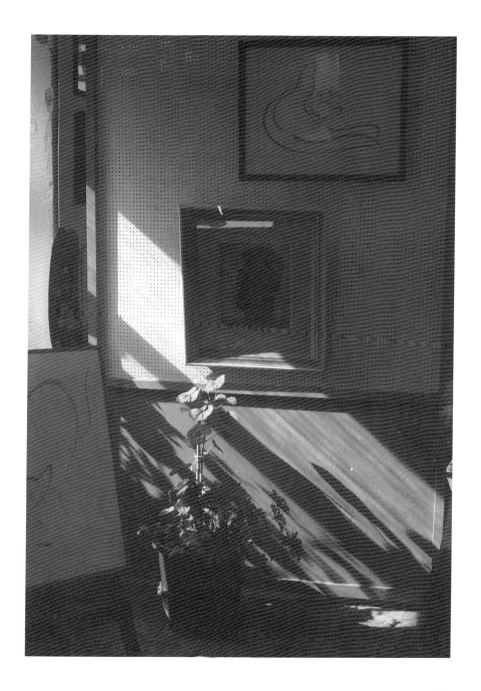

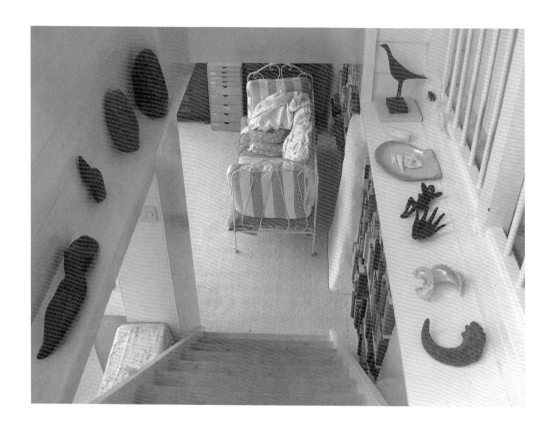

▲ Stairs with Breon
O'Casey Bronze Bird,
Max Barrett Delabole
Slate nude, Fanzani
stone Whistling Men
and Bird Spirit 2009
▶ Tate, St Ives, Roger
Hilton 'Oi, Yoi, Yoi.'
2006

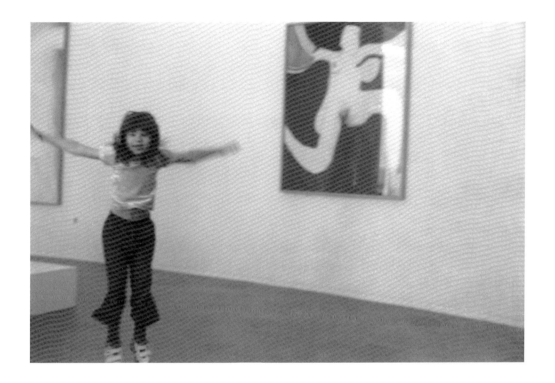

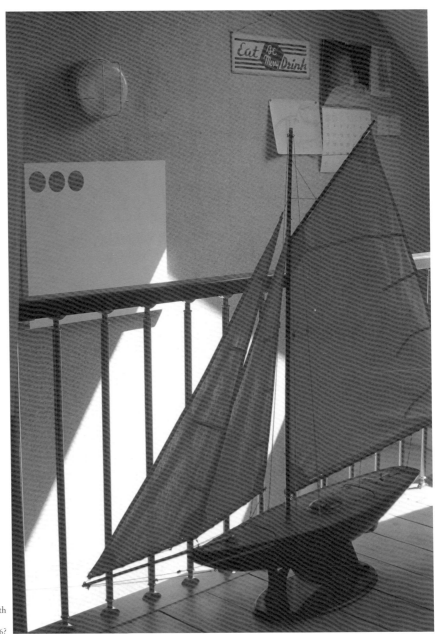

▲ Designer's Studio,
Carrack Dhu 2009
▶ Wedding, Plymouth
Brethren Meeting
House, Barnoon 1986?

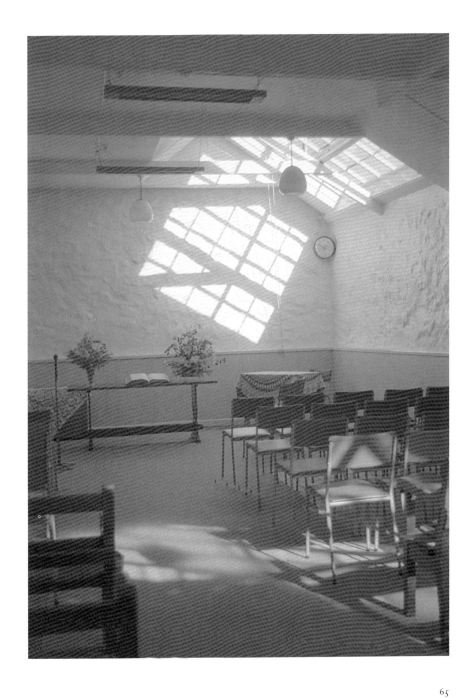

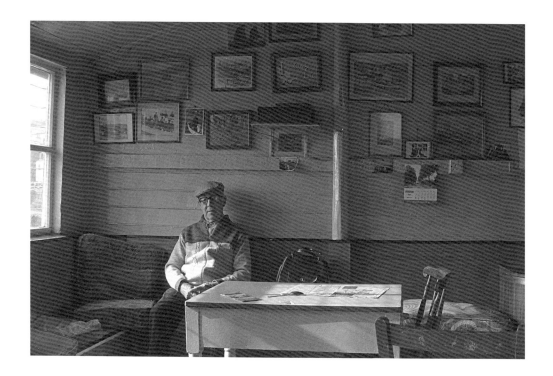

▲ Edgar Humphries,
Shamrock Lodge 1985
▶ Paynter's, the Wharf
1990

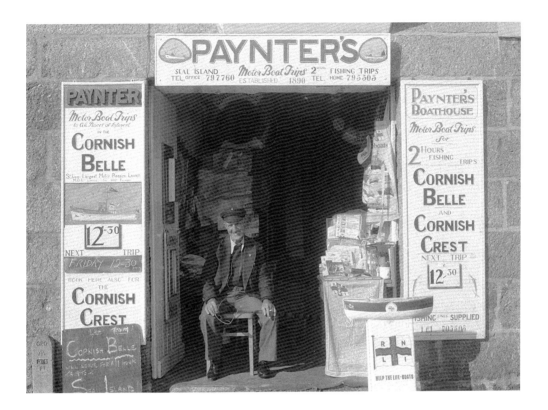

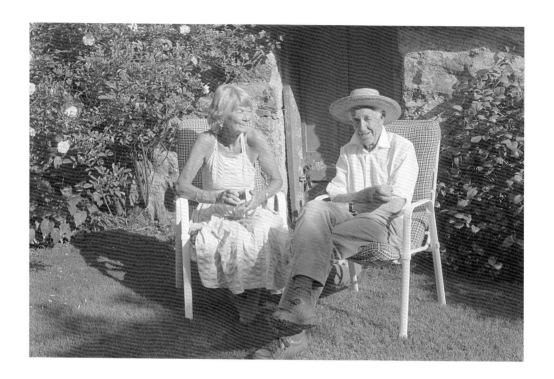

▲ Dr Roger Slack and
Janet Slack 1987?
▶ Rose Hilton 1987

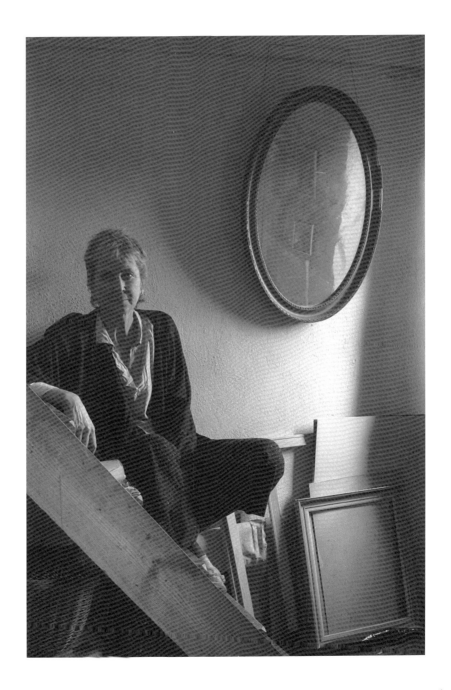

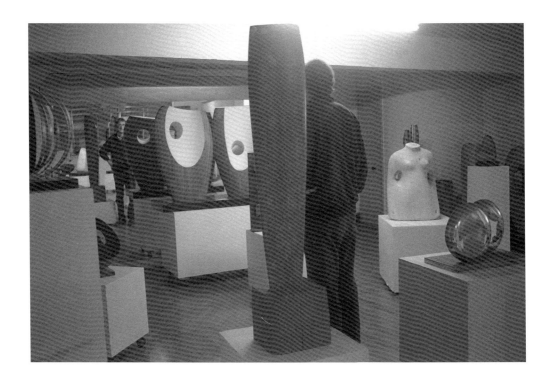

▲ Norman Pollard, with
Barbara Hepworth
sculptures 1985
▶ Bob Devereux,
Salthouse Gallery
1986

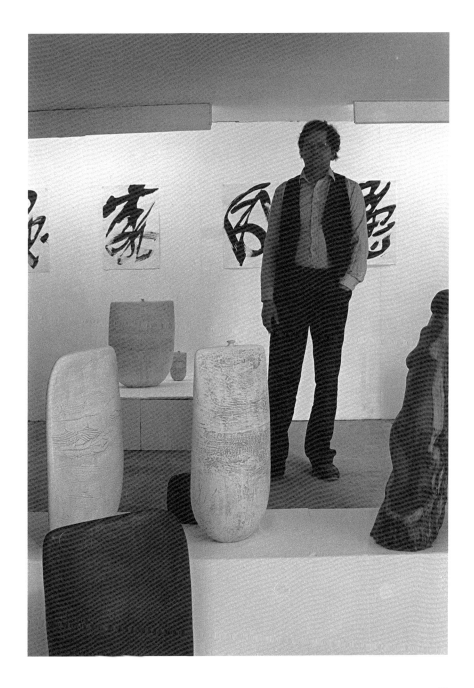

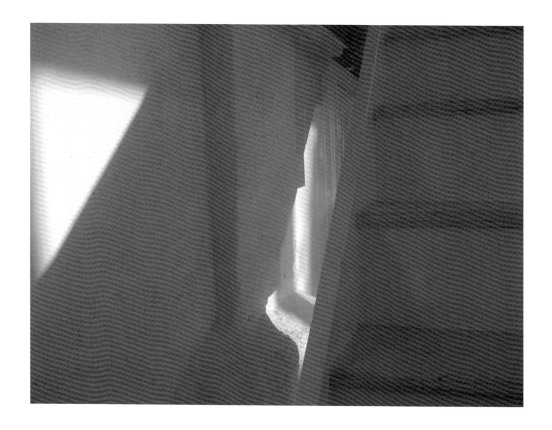

▲ Dawn, Ann Kelley's
Studio 2009
▶ Stennack School
1985

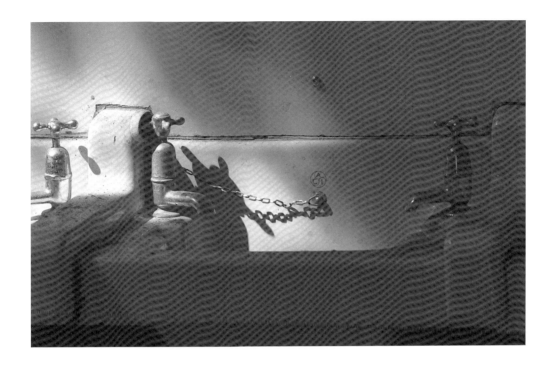

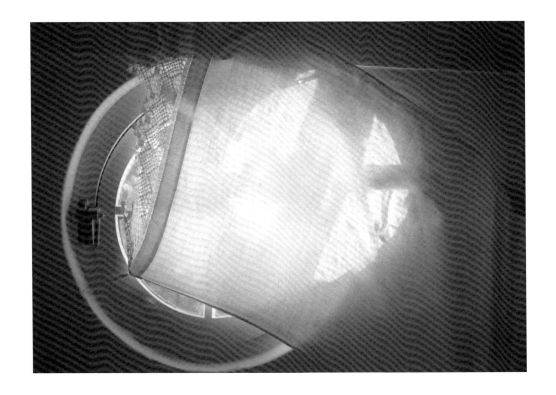

▲ Bathroom window
2007
▶ Wire stars 2009

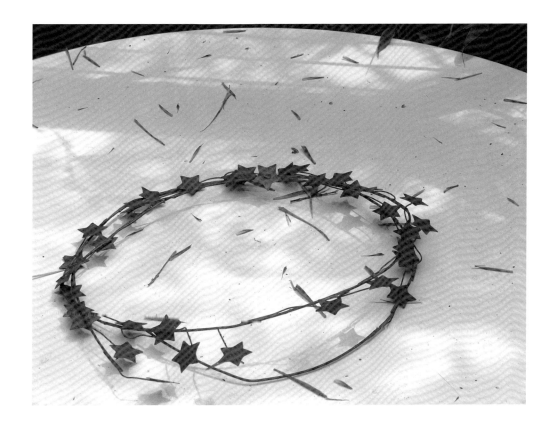

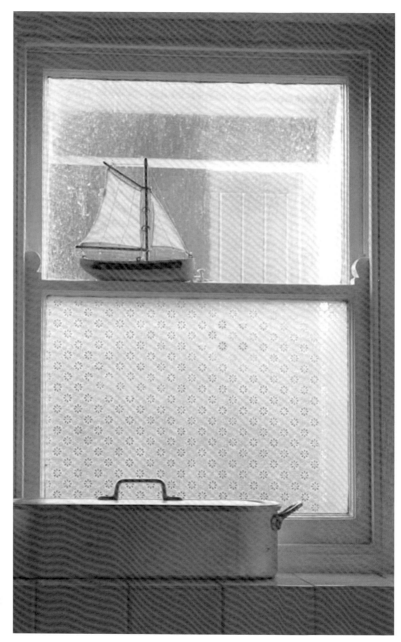

▲ Kitchen 5 Bowling
Green 1979
▶ Christmas 4
Bowling Green 2008

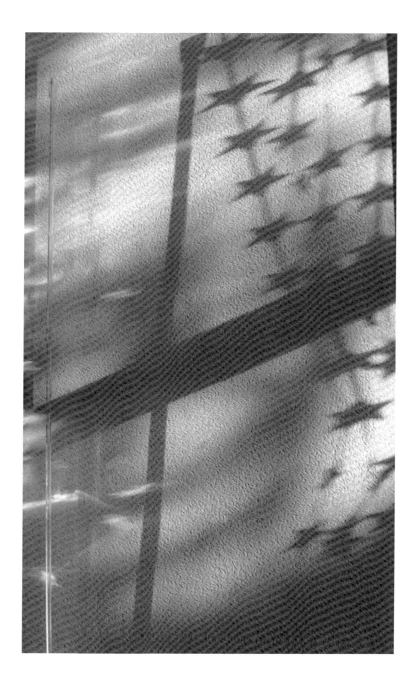

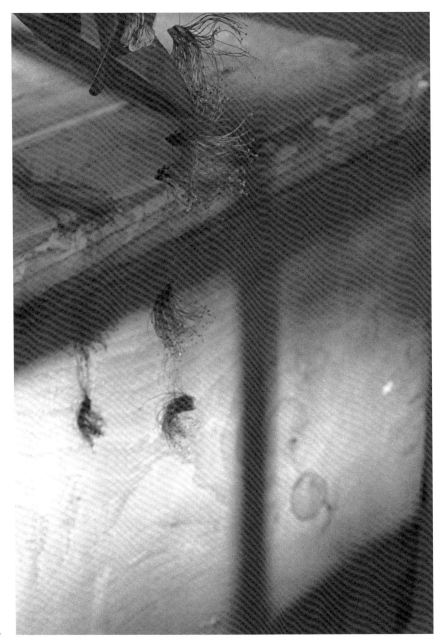

▲ Seeds 2001
▶ Ivy Skeleton 2009

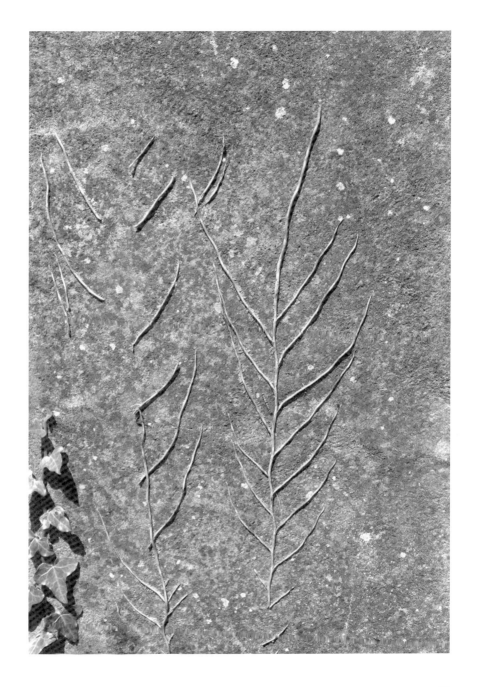

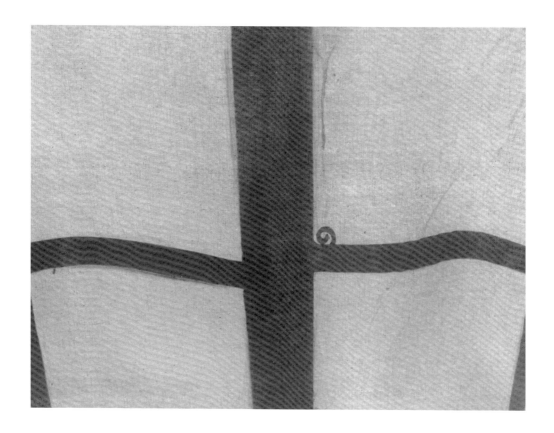

▲ Latch 2007
▶ Embroidered
curtain 2009

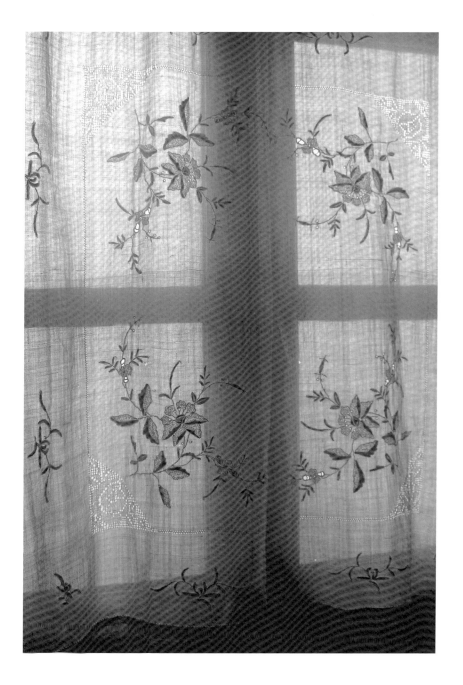

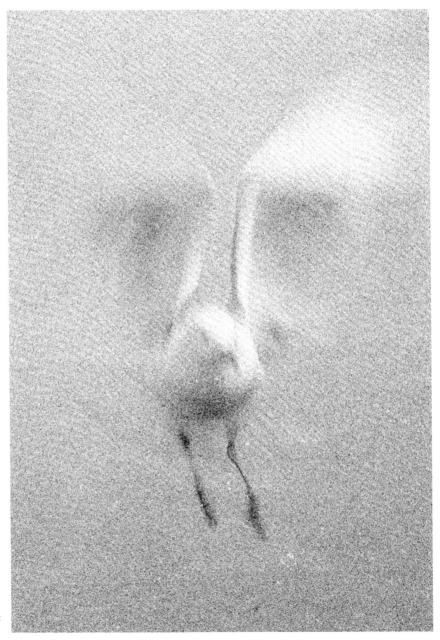

▲ Plunging Gull 1985
▶ Feathers 2009

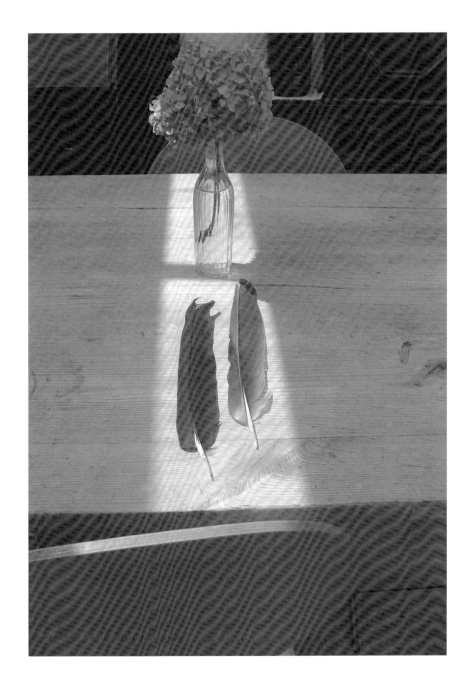

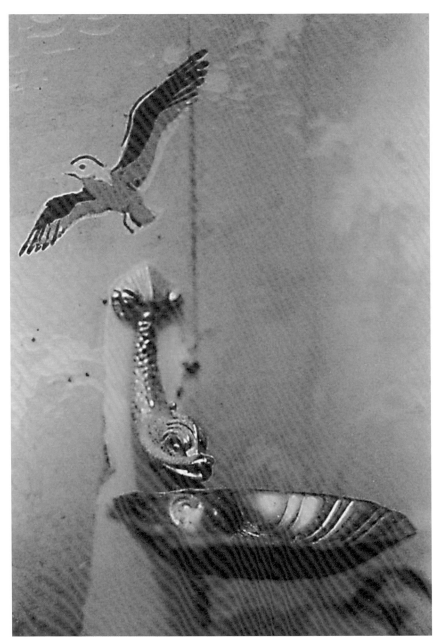

▲ Soap Dish 1990
▶ Dolly in bath 1998

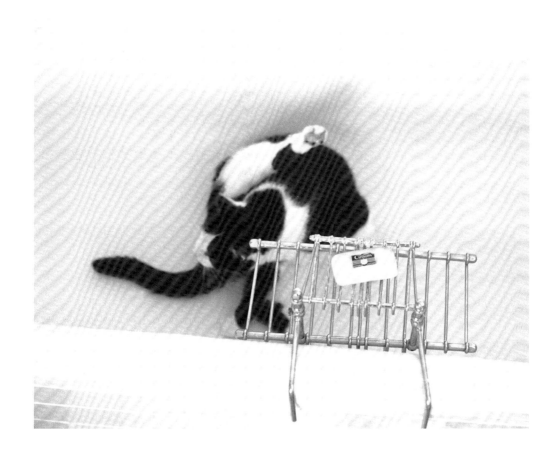

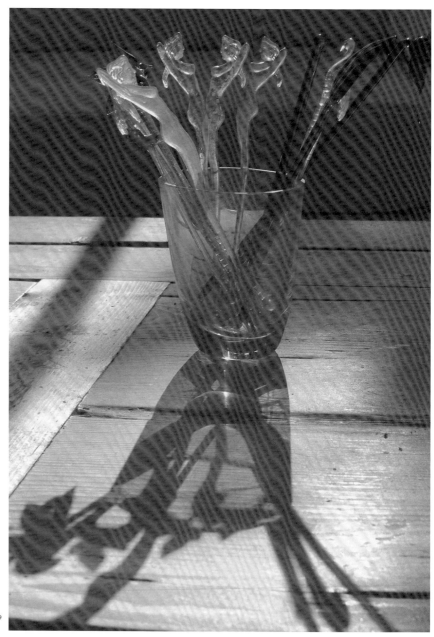

▲ Cocktail sticks 2009
▶ Wire basket 2001

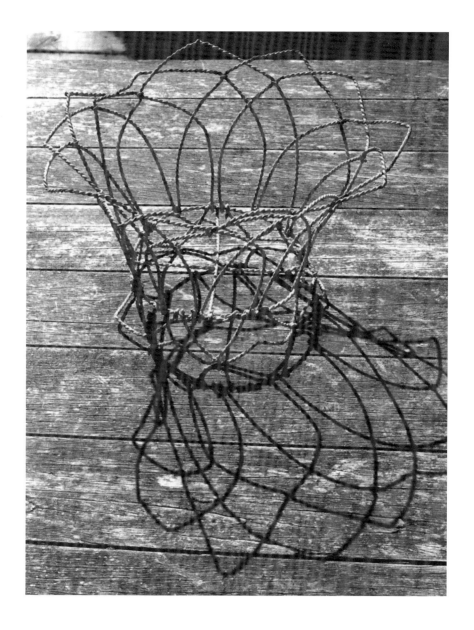

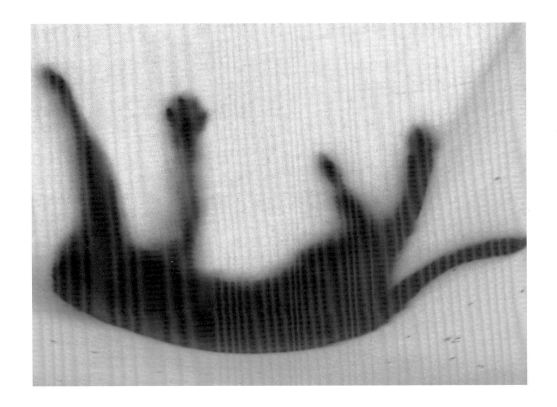

▲ Cat in canvas canopy
2008
▶ Hand ceramic dish
2009

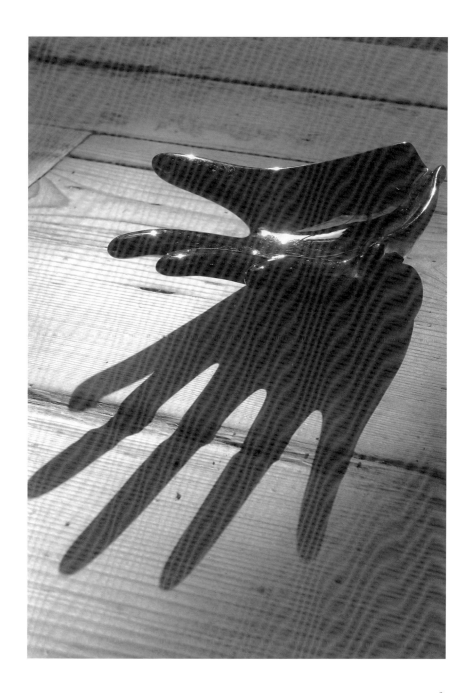

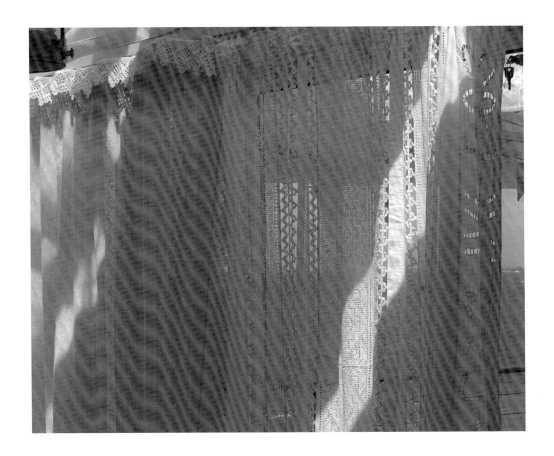

▲ Drawn thread curtain
2009
▶ Shell curtain 2000

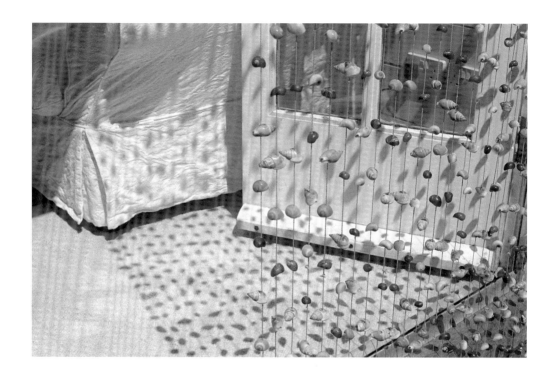

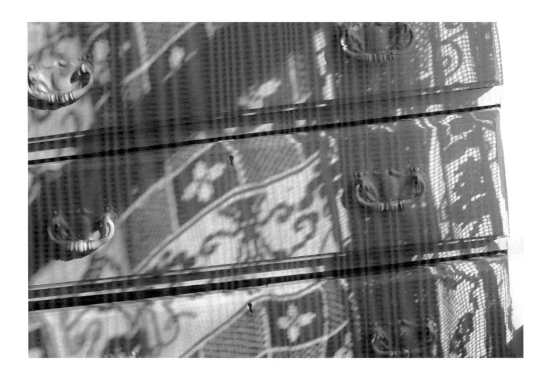

▲ Bowling Green chest
2007
▶ Paper blind and shell
curtain 2006

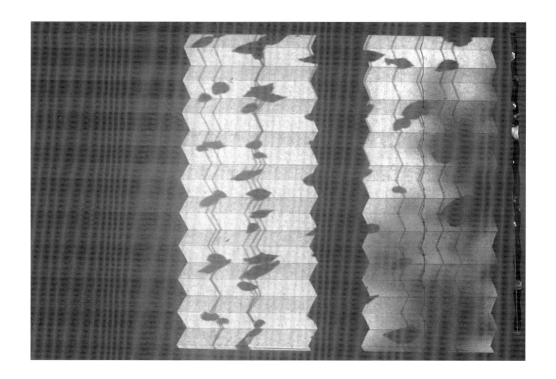

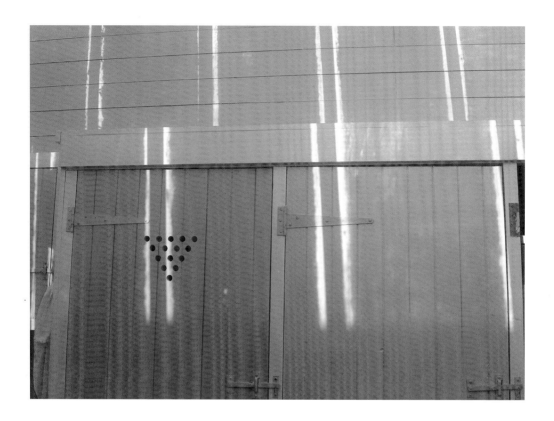

▲ One and All larder 2008
▶ Brian Ilsley mirror 2007

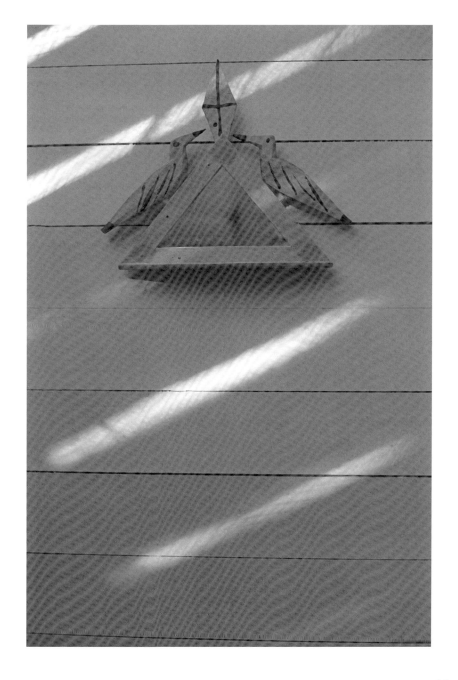

ACKNOWLEDGEMENTS

My thanks to the very generous people who supplied memories of their time in St Ives: Rosamunde Pilcher, the late Sir Terry Frost, and especially Angela, the widow of the late Brian Barron. Many thanks to Helen Dunmore and her publisher for the poem Beautiful Today (*Glad of These Times,* Bloodaxe 2007) and Sylvia Kantaris for the poem The Light at St Ives (*The Sea at the Door,* Octopus). Thanks to DM Thomas for allowing me to quote from his Foreword to *Born and Bred* (Cornwall Books 1988)

And thank you to those people who took the time to write to me and whose words haven't been included: Andrew Lanyon; Trevor Corser; Lady Carol Holland; Marion Whybrow; Martin Val Baker; E. V. Thompson; Harding Laity; Dawn Voice-Cooper and Eric Ward. Thanks also to Gavin MacDougall of Luath Press for enduring faith in my work, and Peter Bennett for the book design.

I'm grateful to my husband Robert Marshall, my daughter Caroline Kelley-Foreman, Mark Foreman, and photographer Ron Sutherland for helping choose the images.

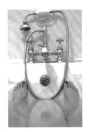

▲ Self portrait 2000